GOD
BROUGHT ME
THROUGH

GOD
BROUGHT ME
THROUGH

TERRANCE J. MCCLAIN, PHD

XULON PRESS

Xulon Press
2301 Lucien Way #415
Maitland, FL 32751
407.339.4217
www.xulonpress.com

Printed in the United States of America.

ISBN-13: 978-1-6312-9411-2

Dedication

I dedicate this book to anyone who has struggled with any form of sin and felt defeated time and time again. This book is designed to bring you comfort and hope that you can be victorious.

I dedicate this book to anyone who has experienced the weight of sin by guilt, shame, and the like, and feel as though you cannot move forward with your life. Your past does not dictate your future. As cliché as it may sound, God has a plan for your life, and it doesn't end with defeat!

I dedicate this book to anyone who has believed the lies of the enemy about your identity. My story, as you will read, was permeated with lies that I believed about my life. I did not realize, nor did I know, what God had to say about me.

And finally, a special dedication to all who have struggled with same-sex attraction and have not been able to find freedom. My story is about this and how God brought victory in an area that I did not think could be possible. God truly gave me beauty for ashes.

Table of Contents

Acknowledgments

With special thanks:

- To God for allowing me to have such a powerful testimony! He allowed me to have and share this testimony for a time such as this. Without Him, I could do nothing! He has given me hope and a future that is beyond my wildest dreams!
- To my beautiful wife, who is a mighty warrior for Christ. She has loved me completely for who I am. I prayed for a woman like her, not realizing that she would be more than even what I could ask for. She allows me to walk in my purpose and share my testimony that many women would not be able to bare. I praise God for her.
- To my mother and father for instilling values and integrity in me. I thank my mother for her powerful and effective prayers for all of her children and especially me. I thank her for raising me in church and holding on to the faith. I thank my father for breaking generational curses of his past to be a father that he never had. I thank him for also teaching me the value of hard work.
- To Breanna Roundtree for never being afraid to speak the truth of God's Word to me. I thank her for being there when I needed her the most. She will always and forever be part of my testimony.
- To Pastor Marie Nuttall and New Jerusalem Baptist Church. Thank you for allowing God to use you to bring deliverance in my life. Thank you for introducing me to the power of the

Holy Spirit. Without you and this church, I would not be as strong in the faith as I am. This book does not contain even half of the things I experienced in this church. I will always be thankful to you.

- To Pastor Anthony V. Monroe and First Lady Monroe and Greater St. Johns Church of God in Christ. I have never experienced a church and a pastor's love the way I have at this church. You were used to usher in the fulfillment of my testimony, and I am indebted to you and this family. I would not have made it through without you.

- To Pastor Chris and Chelsey Larson and New Life Fellowship Church. I thank you for allowing me to be myself and break out of stereotypes and walk in the calling that God has over my life. Our story is yet being written.

A Word from Aundreia

"What's it like? Aren't you like...nervous or something?" These were the first words spoken by a dear friend of mine when I told her my husband had been delivered from a life of homosexuality. As it turns out, many people in my life had the exact same questions. At first, I would get offended and very defensive. It was easy for me to see that God had radically delivered Terrance from homosexuality, and I couldn't understand why others had a hard time believing the same. But as I continued to walk in covenant relationship with my husband, I realized that he and I are living a narrative that very few people have the courage to talk about.

Revelations 12:11 says that we can have confidence in knowing that we will prevail over the things that try to overtake us in life because of the blood that Jesus shed for us on the Cross and by the powerful word of our testimony. As you read this testimony, I hope that you are encouraged to bring the strongholds that may be trying to overtake your life into submission under our all mighty and all-powerful Heavenly Father.

Terrance's story is an intimate picture of the messy yet beautiful exchange that occurs when we bring our brokenness before our Heavenly Father. God has used this story to remind me that He is a loving father and can take the ugliest things in our lives and make them beautiful. I pray that this story encourages you and reminds you that the same redeeming love that restored my husband is strong enough to tear down any stronghold that you face.

With love,
Aundreia

So if the Son sets you free, you will be free indeed.

John 8:36

Introduction

The purpose of this book is to share my testimony about how God brought me through one of the most challenging aspects of my life. I will discuss many facets of my life that are scary, difficult to talk about, and counter-cultural to modern opinion. The major theme of this book addresses my journey through homosexuality, or same-sex attraction, and how God allowed me to experience this in light of His redemptive plan for my life.

Not only will I discuss this major theme, but I will also address deep-rooted issues that contributed to my journey. I am aware that many who read this may not agree with many of the things that will be stated. However, I do ask that you allow yourself, should this offend you, to be open to a different narrative that I do not believe is often heard.

I will take you from my childhood all the way through marriage. As I begin to dissect each part of my life, I pray that my words communicate a positive message of redemption. My goal is to not portray anyone in a negative light. Many, if not all, names were removed to protect their identities. While my desire is to speak the truth regarding my testimony, I will not provide any explicit descriptions about my experiences.

I praise and thank God for my testimony and for allowing me to experience what I have. I do not by any means believe that my experience is representative of the experience of anyone else who has dealt with or is dealing with homosexuality. But I do believe that my story will provide some perspective to the Christian church, and to those who have professed Christ as their Savior and who are currently struggling with homosexuality or know someone who is. I do not provide a step-by-step process for defeating homosexuality because that process does not exist. I cannot guarantee that just because you read this book, you will be able to change other people's perspectives about homosexuality and their faith. I can promise that you will encounter a narrative that is different from what you may have heard before.

My prayer is that every person who reads this will experience the presence of God. What does that mean? It means that if you are reading this book, I pray that the Holy Spirit will be in your presence and that you will see, through my life, what a Holy God can do if you give your life completely and totally to Him. I believe that Jesus died for any and every sin. That means that He died for every ugly, disgusting, shameful, and cringing sin that we could ever encounter. My God can break the chains of any stronghold in your life. I pray that you receive my testimony with Grace. Thank you for taking the time to read my story.

CHAPTER 1

My Childhood

My childhood was not a terrible one. I grew up in a two-parent household that, comparatively speaking, was rare for my neighborhood. I was the youngest child and only son. For the most part, I grew up as a joyful individual. I attended a Baptist church throughout my childhood, and the church served as my safe place at times. I spent a good portion of each week at the church and loved being there. Academically, I excelled in school and was often liked by my teachers. Life was good.

While much of my life was happy, it was not without tribulations. Something I know for sure is that the enemy does not wait until we are developed adults to come against our destiny. He begins as early as possible to plant seeds of doubt, hurt, discouragement, disappointment, and more. I believe this is exactly what he did to me (John 10:10).

Words are extremely powerful. The Word of God says that life and death are in the power of the tongue (Prov. 18:21). But as a child, I did not realize that words spoken to me had the power to alter my life. For as long as I can remember, homosexuality was spoken over me. I recall numerous occasions when homosexual remarks or gestures were made to me or in my presence. They came in every form and from every source in my life. Even those I held dear often participated in this. I was the target of homosexual slanders in my home from my family, at church, and at school.

I was not a masculine individual. I did not fit the mold of what a Black man should look like or how he should behave. I did not like sports. I did not like the oversexualization of women. I recall having crushes on girls at my school, but I was not the stereotypical young Black man. Because of this, I was often shunned by my community. I had trouble making same-sex friendships because of my differences, as I was not chosen to be someone's friend because I was not seen as manly enough. Therefore, my group of friends were few and often female.

I was bombarded by phrases like "be a man," "don't be a wimp," and "boys don't cry," as well as various other sayings about manhood that are spoken to little boys. It was incredibly difficult for me to hear these things, especially because many of these concepts were contrary to the Word of God.

I also found myself constantly fighting, both physically and mentally. Growing up as a boy who was labeled as "gay" was not easy. I was often bullied by many of the guys at my school, which resulted in many fights. I was often an easy target for boys who needed to stroke their egos and exert their masculinity. This happened not only at school, but also in the church. Mentally, I found myself beginning to question my identity and my sexuality. I was also easy prey for guys who wanted to experiment with their sexuality. As a child, I was often the target of sexual misconduct from boys my age. At times, I was blamed for being the one to push myself on them. This pushed me further away from boys and same-sex friendships. Unknown to my parents, I spent much of my childhood in shame and fear.

While I felt the safest at home with my family, I was still full of anxiety because I felt I didn't have a truly safe place. Even my family sometimes made homosexual slanders toward me. The slanders from my family were the most hurtful ones. I knew they said things about me behind my back. I knew that my mannerisms often embarrassed them. They were also vocal in their thoughts about my sexuality, often declaring that I would grow up to be gay.

My relationship with my father holds much weight for me. My father wasn't terrible. He, like many other American fathers, was not aware of the importance of being emotionally present. My father was not fortunate enough to have his father in his life, and as a result, he was introduced to fatherhood with few positive or godly examples. He fulfilled his role as a father by providing food and financial support to his family. He was a good father in that we never lacked for material things. I do believe that because of his upbringing, he did not always know how to connect with his children. As a child, I often felt neglected. The older I became, the more distant my father became with me. At the time, I did not understand why. There were many times I wished I had an intimate connection with my father, but I did not. I often had many extracurricular activities that I participated in, but they were supported and attended by only my mother. This was usually because my father had to work. But many people thought that my mother was a single parent. I felt that I did not have many male role models in my life, and this left me with many voids in my life. I did not realize this in the moment, but much of our identity is tied to our fathers. I know this because God has chosen the role of father to describe His relationship with us as His children (1 Cor. 8:6). The role of the father is critical for a child's development, and it was for mine. My father was a good father, but there were many things I lacked emotionally and spiritually.

As a young child, I dreamed of one day having a wife of my own and being a father. I desired to one day love someone unconditionally and to have the same in return. Of course, this desire was not rooted in Christ. Rather than wanting a marriage so that God could be glorified,

I wanted this for selfish reasons. Ultimately, I wanted to be married so that someone could love me and fill the void that I had in my current situations. I also wanted to be able to love my children the way I felt I was not loved. This, like my idea of marriage, was also not rooted in Christ and was an avenue to fill a void. I was not whole but very broken from life experiences. My desire for marriage and children was always in the back of my mind. However, when you are constantly told that you are gay, it makes you think differently about things. I felt that my life wasn't meant for marriage because I was "gay."

Due to the constant slanders in my life, I found myself living with anxiety because I was terrified of being called gay, being picked on, or getting into a fight. This literally destroyed the very fiber of my being. My identity was obliterated, and I did not have the chance to really learn who I was. I did not realize then, but the enemy had a desire to steal my voice. This did many things to me. The first was it made me a people-pleaser, although I didn't realize this until many years later. I constantly sought the approval of others because I felt that much of life was met with disapproval. Just to feel loved and appreciated, I began to do anything people wanted.

The second thing that resulted from this part of my life was the need for male approval and intimacy. I believe that men seek approval from other men. The same was true for me. I began to seek approval in any way that I could. I recall a group of guys who wanted to teach me "how to be a man." Of course, this included all materialistic and shallow concepts of manhood. They showed me how to walk, talk, and sexualize women. While I tried my best to fit this mold, it quickly faded away because it was inconsistent with who I was. However, not having male friends made me willing to do whatever it took to have some form of male approval. This was my gateway into sexual experiences with men for which I was completely unprepared.

The outcome that these experiences had on me, as I previously mentioned, destroyed my identity and self-confidence. I did not know who I was. To be honest, at that time, my identity was in what others thought of me. And what most people said is that I was someone who was gay. My identity was rooted in the opinions of others rather than in God (Col. 3:2). This meant that my life was not my own. As I entered my teenage years, I was lost and in a dark place.

Summary and Key Themes

My childhood, while not completely unpleasant, was filled with attacks from the enemy. When I was very young, the enemy began to destroy my character and to strip me of my identity. He used people and words to shape my future. The relationships that I had with my father, mother, siblings, family, church, community, and school all came together to form my identity. Unfortunately, many of my interactions were destructive to my identity and character because I did not fit the mold of masculinity as prescribed by those around me. These interactions paved the way for the adolescent, teenage, and adult years of my life.

Key themes discussed in this chapter are:

- **The Power of Words.** The Power of Words is so important to a child's character and identity. We must be careful with the words we speak over our children, family, friends, and loved ones. Words can literally be life or death to them.
- **The Relationship with a Father.** The relationship with a father is also critical to a child's growth. Many of our deep-rooted issues stem from the relationships we have with our fathers.
- **The Role of Masculinity.** The role of masculinity is very present in the lives of young boys and men. We must be careful that we do not take on the world's idea of what masculinity looks like. Rather, we should turn to the Word of God as our guide to defining masculinity.

Key Scriptures

Death and life are in the power of the tongue, and those who
love it will eat its fruits.
Proverbs 18:21

The thief comes only to steal and kill and destroy. I came
that they may
have life and have it abundantly.
John 10:10

Yet for us there is one God, the Father, from whom are all
things and for
whom we exist, and one Lord, Jesus Christ, through whom are all
things and through whom we exist.
1 Corinthians 8:6

Set your minds on things that are above, not on things that
are on earth.
Colossians 3:6

CHAPTER 2

My Adolescent and Teenage Years

The emotional trauma that I experienced as a child was very damaging to my self-esteem and the core of who I was. Beginning in my early childhood, I became keenly aware of how others perceived me. I realized that no matter how nice I was or what I had to offer, many times, the first thought that ran through a person's mind upon meeting me was "I wonder if he is gay." This became somewhat of a paranoia for me. I did not want to meet new people or be social. I developed a strong sense of fear of what others thought about me. These were all building blocks for stealing my voice and my identity. During this time, I knew nothing about placing my identity in Christ. In my mind and in my environment, how others perceived me was everything. I endured many microaggressions from my family about the way I should behave so that people wouldn't assume I was gay. As a result of this trauma, I found myself spending more time with older adults simply because children were incredibly mean to me, though being with adults was not without their ridicule.

What I did not recognize at the time was that my voice was very important. But because of the emotional trauma I experienced in my childhood and through middle school and high school, I was afraid to be who God called me to be. I was afraid to operate in the gifts that God had bestowed upon me. I chose to hide, and this persisted through much of my early adulthood. The enemy was doing his best to destroy my very being.

Spiritual Life

During my middle school years, I became really engaged in Christ. I loved the idea of living a life that was centered in Christ and was excited about attending church. Many days, I would sit at the front of the service to encourage my pastor. I loved attending our youth classes that were developed for us to learn more about Christ. I also became extremely engaged with other ministries within the church as well. I was a member of the usher board, youth choir, and praise/interpretative dance group. At this point in my life, I was also participating in other extracurricular activities like Tae Kwon Do. As a child, I always loved action movies that involved fighting. As I reflect on this, maybe I enjoyed this so much because it was a form of defense for me. Often, it was a place of escape and a way to release anger and stress. However, my passion was to be in the church, so I made this my priority and decided to quit all other activities.

As I reflect back on this, I believe I was extremely genuine in my pursuit of God. I also believe that, as sure as I was about my pursuit of God, the enemy was just as sure in trying to keep me from my destiny. Within my specific church, I did not see a culture of following Christ among the youth. It was not popular for children my age to be on fire for God. I often found myself in isolation because I wanted to be about the things of God rather than about the things that would make me popular. For a while, I was able to hold my own and not give in to the peer pressure of adolescence. But despite my efforts, I was unable to resist because I longed for a place to find community and a place where I would fit in with my peers.

There were many things about the spiritual walk with Christ that I did not know. My church did not teach children about the tricks and schemes of the enemy. And because of my lack of knowledge, I found myself vulnerable to them. The combination of my childhood struggles and my continual need for approval provided an open door for sin to enter into my life. As I began to experience sin, a slow death took place in my spiritual walk and connection with my Savior. Romans 8:6 states, "For the mind of the flesh is death..." The more I continued to live in sin, the more I wanted and desired to chase my fleshly desires and the things of the world. By "the things of the world," I mean my desires for material gain, status, approval, and affection apart from God.

Struggle with Sin

At the age of eight, I was introduced to sexual immorality. As a child, I was around children who were older than me. I looked up to these individuals because I wanted to fit in. Though I knew right from wrong, I was conflicted (Matt. 26:41). Because the label of "gay" was placed on me so early in my life, I always felt the need to justify my sexuality. In addition, my environment did not make it easy for me to walk away from sexual immorality. Many of my sexual participations were not by choice, as I was bullied and threatened physically to participate. Because they were older than me, I knew I would not win a fight if I chose to resist them. Thus, I began to participate in sexual activities and came to enjoy the pleasures of sin. Thankfully, by the time I was in middle school, I was removed from this environment and later was able to focus on God, which I mentioned previously.

Middle School

For middle school, I started at a new school and was able to essentially begin with a clean slate. I moved to a new middle school by choice because I wanted a better education for myself. I attended school in the district that my grandmother lived in, as it was easy for me to go to her house after school. Now older, I chose to attend school where I lived. At this new school, I was exposed to new peers, and I was able to somewhat start a new life. However, I did not realize that sin would follow me wherever I went. I did not deal with the scars of my childhood and had no one with whom I felt safe talking about my childhood. In middle school, I continued to participate in sexual activities, often to prove my masculinity. During this time, my friends introduced me to porn, and I began to explore sexual immortality through self-pleasure. These were gateway sins to what would later be my greatest struggle.

Throughout middle school, there were many instances where male students would make slanderous remarks or sexual gestures toward me. I continued to struggle with same-sex relationships and found I was able to make female friends much easier. I longed to have male friends, but due to my mannerisms, I was never seen as one of the guys. I recall a time when I rode the bus to school and the males on the bus ridiculed me and chanted homosexual slurs. I specifically remember that a girl whom I thought was my friend joined in with the guys. She said she participated only because everyone else was doing it. I remember going to the library and crying until school started. I was so devastated that someone I thought was my friend turned on me so quickly. Sadly, this was not a one-time thing; I continued to have many more experiences like this.

I also recall having many physical fights because guys tried to bully me to puff up their own masculinity. I never told my parents about the many fights I was involved in over the course of elementary and middle school. It was hard for me to be around guys. I developed a sense of fear around them. I was always on guard and began to lose trust in people overall. I lived in fear that at any moment, I would have to fight someone to protect myself. This was a very tough time in my life.

Something else started to take place in my life around this time as well. I began to question my sexuality more. As I mentioned in the first chapter, homosexuality was spoken over my life for as long as I could remember. I recall sitting in my room and asking myself if I was truly gay and perhaps did not know it. I contemplated how my mannerisms reflected what most considered to be signs of homosexuality. However, my true feelings did not match what others believed about me. The more I thought about this, the more I became angry and thought it would be easier to just be what everyone called me to be. I wondered why God would make me like this and why I had to struggle with it. Left unchecked, my thoughts continued to manifest through time. I had become addicted to pornography and began to watch strictly same-sex pornography, which led to more sexual immorality through self-pleasure. In my mind, I truly believed that my personal secret would never touch anyone else. I soon came to realize I was wrong.

I felt like I was living in a world of darkness. I was consumed by my sins and could not figure out how to overcome them. In my church environment, people did not often share what their struggles were because of fear of gossip and other people's views of them being tarnished. On the outside, I appeared to be a kid full of life and joy, but on the inside, I was consumed by darkness. At the age of thirteen, my sin caught up with me. I had my first same-sex experience with a guy who was really close to me. He was one of the few male friends I had, and I was willing to do anything to keep him as my friend. Unfortunately, I came to realize he was my friend for the purpose of manipulation and sexual experience. His main goal was to use me as an opportunity to experiment with his sexuality. However, I cannot place complete blame on him, as I had already been dabbling in same-sex pornography. The desires were already in place; I just needed an opportunity. This experience marked me for the next five years of my life. I had many emotions going through my head after this experience. The first was that I was sure I was going to hell. I grew up in church, and homosexuality was a great sin in my community. At one point, I was doing so well to pursue God, and then it seemed it was all taken away in one moment. The second thought was my feelings about the experience. Did I enjoy this sexual experience with a male? Did this experience officially make me gay? I wasn't sure about any of these things. The third thought was betrayal. Immediately after this experience, the guy I interacted with told me he did not really enjoy this experience like he thought he would and that we were never to speak of this experience again. I was sworn to secrecy. From this point on, he was done with me. I felt so betrayed because I was going through a very critical time in my life, and he was the only person I felt I could confide in. I felt that without him, I had no one I could trust to tell my fears and hopes and dreams. The combination of these things continued to lead me down a dark path.

Now that I had been exposed to same-sex interactions, my mind went on a whirlwind. I quickly realized that I could no longer look at men the same and often saw them as sexual objects. I also did not feel comfortable expressing any of these things within my church community for fear that my and my family's reputation would be tarnished because of my current struggle. The only thing I knew to do was to keep this to myself, believing I would be able to conquer my sin alone. During this time, I also prayed. Every time I thought an unclean thought, I covered myself in prayer. Eventually, the thoughts subsided, and I was able to have some peace in my life. But although I was able to suppress my desire to be physical with men, I still longed for someone to confide in. Keeping this big secret was extremely difficult for a thirteen-year-old.

High School

Entering high school was much like middle school. I went to a new high school in a new district and had to make friends all over again. I moved to a new school district for many of the same reasons that I moved school districts for middle school: I wanted more opportunities. Yet again, I experienced ridicule and harsh treatment from my peers. People often voiced that they did not like me because of the clothes I wore and wouldn't engage with me. I was keenly aware that many male groups did not want me in their inner circles because of fear of association. On top of all this, I was still dealing emotionally with my same-sex experience and was beginning to realize that it had completely changed me. My high school was very open to sexual preferences, specifically for women. However, for men, it was still a touchy subject. Seeing same-sex relationships between women so openly acceptable at my school reawakened my desire to be with a male. My prayer life began to decrease, and thus my passions began to rage. Much of my freshmen year was a blur. I was at a new school and looking for ways to fit in. I was often scared to go to school because of fear of bullying, which often led to fighting. Fighting was never something I enjoyed, so entering an environment not knowing if I would be safe was extremely difficult. The only place I felt I fit in was my high school's gospel choir. Interestingly enough, I quickly discovered that while this was a gospel choir, many of us struggled with the idea of holiness and what it meant to be Christ-like in a world that was very much opposite to what we were taught. I also found that many of the men in this choir also struggled with homosexuality. Though I was not involved in their lives, I was able to observe these things. Seeing this brought some confusion to my mind. This was the first time I had seen people living a lifestyle that was completely opposite to the Word of God and what I was taught while still appearing to have an intimate relationship with God. Seeds of doubt entered my mind, and the thought that this was possible for me was birthed.

By the end of my freshmen year, I met a friend. She was someone I connected with and was also the very first person I was able to confide in about my same-sex experience. She too struggled with same-sex attraction. For the first time, I felt I had someone to feel safe with. At the time, it was everything I needed. Keeping my secret for over a year had been one of the hardest things I had to do. However, she was not the right person to confide in because rather than push me to Christ for His help, she helped me become more comfortable with the idea of living a life with same-sex attraction. My relationship with her opened the door to new experiences with guys, which fed into my lust. I began to sink deeper and deeper into my sinful nature. All of this was taking place while I was trying my best to cleave to God. My sin continued to place a wedge between my Savior and me. I felt defeated and overwhelmed. The hope I had acquired through prayer was no longer there. I also never heard the testimonies of others and how they had overcome. I believe the Word of God is true in that we overcome by the blood of the lamb and the word of our testimony (Rev. 12:11). I was not accustomed to hearing about the testimonies of what God had done for others, and I surely did not hear testimonies from anyone who struggled with same-sex attraction. My hope had all but faded away.

I spent many days reflecting and crying because, as a child, I dreamed of being married and having children of my own. I wanted to love my son in ways that I had wanted so badly to be loved. Like many, I wanted the American dream. But being labeled homosexual made me believe this life was no longer for me. While I struggled with same-sex attraction and tried to come to peace with it, I never believed that being married to the same sex was what God had intended for His people or for me. But despite those underlying beliefs, my hopelessness seemed to become louder and stronger.

My sophomore year was the year of comfort. During this time, I became comfortable with the idea of being homosexual and met friends who supported me in my struggle. Many of these friends also struggled with same-sex attraction, so we found comfort and safety in one another. It was an amazing feeling to be loved and accepted for who I was. I began to accept who I thought I was, and I had a great support system for it.

My junior year was the year I became openly gay to those around me. Though I did not make public announcements, if asked, I would gladly answer in the affirmative. What I found is I received more acceptance for professing my sexuality than I did when I denounced it. My experience was not what I had expected it to be. I thought revealing my sexuality would lead to increased cruelty. However, for me, that was not the case. I began to engage in various relationships with guys throughout the remainder of high school. I particularly enjoyed the chase of getting a guy who was unsure about his sexuality to like me. Often, they were the more masculine guys who were "ladies' men." I became extremely manipulative in my approach and used love and appreciation as a method to enter the hearts of men who I wanted to pursue. More often than not, I was successful. What I did not realize at the time was that God had gifted me with the power of influence. However, rather than operating in my gift for the pursuit of God, I was using it for my own satisfaction and personal gain. I also did not recognize my love for the chase. The manipulation of men who I pursued tapped into a variety of insecurities I had yet to become aware of. The chase provided me with opportunities to fill my void of acceptance and need. By having a guy like me, I felt needed and wanted. Male companionship was something I desperately desired but did not have. The only time I had this was when a man wanted to have sexual relations with me. I did not know love from a man emotionally or even physically outside of perversion.

I believe that no matter how far I walked away from God, He was always there, waiting and calling me back (Jer. 3:14)! Throughout my entire high school career, there was one young lady who spoke truth and the Word of God over my life (Prov. 25:11). She also struggled with same-sex attraction, but I admired her because she fought hard against it. She would often pull me aside and say these words: "Terrance, this is not the lifestyle that God has for you!" This young lady would also encourage me with many other words, but it was that specific sentence that would replay in my mind. Although I did not respond to her in agreement, I kept her words in my heart. I knew deep down inside she was right. As much as I wanted to make peace with the idea of being homosexual, I knew it did not match with the Word of God. Many times, I tried to overcome same-sex attraction and failed miserably. I saw many others who tried and were not successful. While I wanted to grab ahold to God, it just seemed impossible for me. I continued to live the lifestyle I was in and pushed these thoughts to the back of my mind.

My final year of high school was spent focusing on the future, which for me was college. I was excited about attending college because I wanted a more independent life for myself and to have more freedom to explore my sexuality. My mother was a disciplinarian and did not allow me to do whatever I wanted. In hindsight, I praise God for this because I would have gotten myself into more spiritually destructive situations, like many of my friends did. I was accepted to and chose to attend Texas A&M University in College Station, Texas. I was excited and thrilled to be accepted into such a prestigious school. Many people did have concerns about me attending Texas A&M because it was a predominately white school that had a reputation for being conservative.

Many felt I would not be well received because of my sexuality. However, I knew that no matter where I went, I would find others who were like me. I knew I would be okay. What I did not know at the time was that God was actually ordaining my steps (Psalm 37:23).

Summary and Key Themes

This period of my life was critical because it was a time when I wanted to learn more about God and a time when the enemy introduced more sin into my life. Because I was unaware of the full dangers and consequences of sin, I was not prepared to fight the enemy. I also did not have many individuals in my life during this time who were willing to speak the truth. It is important to develop relationships with children during adolescent or teenage years and lead them to the mind of Christ. The enemy is ready and willing to claim the souls of our youth and children. Rather than leaving the spiritual condition of our children to chance, we should be intentional in our relationships with them.

Key themes discussed in this chapter are:

- **Cultivating the spiritual condition of our children.** It is important that, as parents, we cultivate the spiritual condition of our children. If you are a parent, be sure you are involved in the growth of your child's spiritual connection to God and do not depend on others to do it or leave it to chance. It is also wise to create a safe place for your children to allow them to tell you about the things going on in their lives. Without this safe place, they are likely to go to anyone who will receive them, and this may too often be the wrong person.

- **Sin and its devastating grip on the lives of people.** For the wages of sin is death. Sin is powerful, and it separates us from God. We should never underestimate the devasting power of sin. Sin will take you where you never thought you would go and will influence you to do things you never thought you would do. Be very careful, and be sure to guard your heart.

Key Scriptures

Return, O faithless children, declares the Lord; for I am your master;
I will take you, one from a city and two from a family,
and I will bring you to Zion.
Jeremiah 3:14

The steps of a man are established by the Lord, when he delights
in his way.
Psalm 37:23

A word fitly spoken is like apples of gold in a setting of silver.
Proverbs 25:11

Watch and pray that you may not enter into temptation. The
spirit indeed is
willing, but the flesh is weak.
Matthew 26:41

For to set the mind on the flesh is death, but to set the mind on the
Spirit is life and peace.
Romans 8:6

And they have conquered him by the blood of the Lamb and
by the word of their testimony, for they loved not their lives
even unto death.
Revelation 12:11

CHAPTER 3

My College Years

Entering college, I had many goals in mind, but the prevalent one was freedom. Like many freshmen, I was excited for the opportunity to be independent and live on my own. For me, this meant I finally had the chance to explore my sexuality more deeply. As I mentioned in the previous chapter, my mother was protective of me in that I was not allowed to do whatever I wanted. As I began my freshmen journey, I immediately met new friends. For the first time in my life, people actually thought I was cool and wanted to be my friend. They liked me for who I was and did not automatically judge me. I felt I no longer had to fit particular molds of masculinity. I was free of the chains of my community, and I could now be who I wanted to be. For the first time, there were guys in my life who wanted to be just my friend. Up until this point, I had not had many male friendships that were not sexual in nature. It felt wonderful to have guys who simply wanted to be friends. I became extremely social and found my identity in being popular and as someone who people loved. Also during this time, I connected with other guys who were gay, and we formed great bonds with one another. Not only did I have new friends and popularity, but I also had a place within the LGBTQIA community.

I was determined to live a life I knew was opposite of what God declared in His Word, but because of my training as a child, I also knew I should find a church. Thus, within two weeks of being at school, I was on the search for a church home. After visiting two churches, I found a place to call home, New Jerusalem: The Powerhouse of Deliverance. For much of this book, I have chosen to omit names to protect all persons involved. However, because of the positive impact this church had on my life, I have chosen to use the real name. I think I chose this church because I was intrigued by the name. I thought it sounded very cool, and I liked how the word *deliverance* sounded. When I attended my first service, I felt a complete overshadowing of the Holy Spirit. It was quite strange to me because I had never felt the presence of the Lord as strongly as I did in that moment. I also felt a deep sense of conviction regarding my lifestyle that I had not felt before. When I had my very first sexual experience with another male, I felt guilt and shame rather than conviction. But for the first time, I felt a conviction from the Holy Spirit that was second to none (1 Thess. 1:5). While this conviction made me extremely uncomfortable, I enjoyed it! I left that service feeling different. I did not know at the time that God had started a work in me that I could not fathom. I liked the service so much that I wanted to go again. However, I was not ready to go back on my own, so I constantly looked for others to come with me. For a season, this worked. But there came a time when I realized I had to want God more than I wanted someone to be by my side.

Throughout the semester, God began to birth praise and worship within me. I would attend church and could not control my outbursts of praise. I had never done this before. It was actually quite embarrassing. But something on the inside of me could not help but praise God for what He was doing in my life. Every time I went to church, the Holy Spirit would speak to me on the inside and challenge me to give my life to Him. I had never before understood what people meant by "the Holy Spirit spoke to me," but I was now experiencing it firsthand. Sometimes it was an audible voice, and other times it was simply my conscience nudging at me. As the Spirit of God continued to prompt me to give my life to Him, I pondered what this meant. I interpreted it as leaving the life of homosexuality behind me. And to be honest, I wanted it gone. My identity was so rooted in being gay that I saw no way out. As much as I tried to resist God's prompting, I could not. As a result, praise and worship began to pour out of me. After an entire semester of wrestling with God about giving my life to Him, I finally gave in. But I was scared of what this would mean. I did not want to fail or be defeated. I had never known victory in this area of my life.

On my way home for Christmas break after my first semester, I gave my life to Christ. I was alone in my car, and my prayers and dedication were sincere. While I wish I could say that everything from that point on was easy, it certainly was not. When I got home, I made a declaration on Facebook about what God had done for me. However, this declaration was vague at best. Immediately, I received a message from a guy who had become my friend on social media a few months prior. He sent me a message asking what I meant by the post. I was sincere and told him exactly what I meant. To my surprise, this was a trap by the enemy (1 Pet. 5:8). He said he was interested in me and was sad to hear I no longer wanted to live a life of homosexuality. At that moment, my insecurities set in. I couldn't believe that a guy of his caliber wanted to be with someone like me. A guy of my dreams wanted me. My need for approval from a man made me feel vulnerable. I was upset because I couldn't believe that in the moment I decided to give my life to God, the very thing I wanted presented itself. Why couldn't this have happened before I gave my life to Christ? I knew this was the enemy, but I couldn't resist. I gave in and started a relationship with this guy that was not healthy. I did things with him I had never done before. I did not know who I was, and I was completely driven by lust.

Despite my intentional walk away from the Lord, He still took time to minister to me through conviction by the Holy Spirit. I did not have peace in my mind or heart because I knew that I gave my life to God and then walked out on Him. I contemplated who I could reach out to for help. The Holy Spirit reminded me of my friend from high school who spoke truth into my life. At the exact moment I needed it, God provided me with help by bringing her to my mind, and she will forever be part of my testimony. I called her and confessed what I had done. She was kind and loving and walked me through the steps I needed to take to move away from this situation. She prayed with me, and I developed a new resolve for walking with God. I had to make good on my word to my Savior! I prayed and asked God for a way out of the situation. And glory to God, He gave me one. I spoke with this guy and confessed that I could no longer be in the relationship because I had given my life to God. I challenged him by asking if he was willing to be in a relationship with me beyond sexual pleasures, and if he wasn't, then I was done. I knew this was something he would not be willing to do, so I used it as a way to get out of the situation. At the time, I did not have the courage to simply end it. Thankfully, he agreed to end things, and we parted ways. A weight was lifted from me because I had messed up and needed to make good on my promise. I was both excited and ready to come back to the Lord.

I wish I could say that after this fall, I was able to get it together. However, I found myself in another unhealthy situation with a friend from my past (1 Pet. 5:8). I again felt vulnerable and had a sexual experience after confiding in him that I was walking away from a life of homosexuality. This experience made me feel defeated because I fell twice within a short span of time. I couldn't experience victory in this area of my life, and I became more hopeless. But despite my failures, I could not shake the fact that I had given my life to Christ and had to make good on my word. I also learned a very valuable lesson from these experiences: that I had to do whatever it took to get the freedom I wanted. That meant friends, places, and even family had to be removed from my life if they did not push me toward Christ. I had to be completely honest about my shortcomings and not believe I was stronger than I was. These experiences humbled me in a way I had not felt before. On my way back to school, one thing that stayed with me was victory. I would no longer settle for defeat in my life. I had been defeated for so long, and not everything was my doing. The lies, the lack of love, the ridicule, et cetera, were no longer in my life. I resolved that I would *not be defeated*!

When I returned to school for my second semester of freshmen year, the Holy Spirit began to speak to me even more. It was almost like I was talking to someone right in front of me. I had a conversation with God; He let me know it would be hard to move away from a lifestyle I had grown so comfortable with, but it was not impossible. Nothing is impossible for God! The Lord asked me if I was ready to accept the challenge to walk with Him this time. My answer was *yes*. He said so clearly to me, "If you take one step, I'll make two!" Those words were truly life to me.

In January 2009, I made a vow unto the Lord to walk away from homosexuality. About a week or two later, I started showing signs of herpes, and I went to the doctor in complete fear. I could not believe this could happen to me. I was not the most sexually active person I knew. I had hardly done anything with anyone, and the moment I did, I contracted a sexually transmitted disease. I began to pray to the Lord like I had never done before in my life. Needless to say, there were many tears to go along with my prayers. After several tests, the results were negative. I began to praise God from what I like to call "the pit of my belly"! This was most evident when I came to church the following Sunday. And while I was praising Him, many people looked at me in wonder, but at the time, no one could understand my excitement because they did not know my story. Once again, I heard the voice of the Lord ever so clearly. He informed me that this scare was a warning for me to never go back to where He had brought me from. I listened to Him. And I carried on in vow to God.

Although I made a vow unto the Lord, my journey was far from easy. After I made my dedication, I was immediately tested. I ran into several friends from the homosexual community. They asked if I was interested in going to the gay club with them and having fun. I informed them I could not do those things any longer. Of course, they wanted to know why. I told them in a trembling voice that I was following God. They literally laughed and said, "Please don't go all Jesus on us." I could not believe they were so bold as to laugh in my face. In that moment, I again realized that if I truly wanted to be free from homosexuality, I had to get with like-minded individuals who wanted to push me toward faith. I walked away from them and felt my dedication begin to grow.

During this time, I tried to pursue intimate relationships with women. I thought I could let go of homosexuality one day and move on with my life the next. I did not realize I needed to do a lot of work in my life before I would be ready to date women. To be honest, I wanted to date a woman because I wanted to prove wrong those who spoke homosexuality over my life. I thought dating a woman was the answer to my problems or at least would help me overcome my challenges. However, God always blocked these situations and allowed me the time I needed for Him to work in my life.

The first thing God worked on was my mind. My mind was so polluted with sin. And here I was thinking I was a good boy. My mind was filthy, and it needed to be renewed and transformed (Rom. 12:1–2). I could not look at a man without sexualizing him in some way. Every single day, I gave my mind to the Lord. I was reminded of being a teenager and first struggling with homosexual thoughts. Each time a thought would come to me, I would pray and focus on God. It was a discipline. Every day, I gave my thoughts to God. Step by step and day by day, I prayed and gave Him my mind. This was no easy task. There were times I simply wanted to lust over men because it was easy, and it was what I wanted. But I had to fight against the flesh. The second thing God showed me was the company of friends and relationships around me. I knew I should remove people from my past who did not want to push me into my future. However, I was still learning about new relationships and how the enemy can use situations to get you off track. At this time in my life, male relationships were a weakness for me, so I found myself continuing to be tricked.

I continued to experience more and more small temptations. Guys began to boldly approach me to enter into a relationship with them. After some time of resistance, I believe the enemy tried different tactics to persuade me to turn back. I had more and more guys come into my life who outwardly appeared to want to be just friends with me. We would go to parties and drink and have fun. Although I had given one area of my life to God, that being homosexuality, I had not given other aspects of my life to him. I was still drinking and participating in other sexual sins (i.e. pornography). As I indulged in other sins, I found myself slowly drifting back to homosexuality as well. However, because of my experiences, I was determined not to do so. I could not go back to where God had brought me from. I became more vigilant in watching who I allowed in my inner circle as much as I knew how. I was always on guard for the enemy because I knew he was crafty. I kept holding on to the little bit of God I could. Every day, I felt that God was working in my life.

The enemy also remained persistent in my life. The guy I was with shortly after I gave my life to Christ on my way home from my first semester of college wanted to come back into my life. In my mind, I thought I had closed that chapter. His reentrance into my life caused me to experience an extreme amount of guilt because I felt I had left him all alone. I remembered exactly how I felt when I had my first sexual experience with another male and the confusion and hurt I felt as a result of him leaving me. This young man was feeling the same thoughts. He did not have a family environment that supported this life choice, and I felt he needed me. But I knew if I allowed him back into my life, I would go down fast. I had made so much progress, and I could not let this take me back. However, I felt somewhat responsible for how he was feeling. It was one of the hardest decisions I had to make. I had let myself down before and could not go back to my past. I had come too far and had to remain strong. I did not allow communication with him for about five months, after which he contacted me again. I thought he was surely over the situation and only wanted to say hello, but I discovered this was not the case. My responding created a small window of hope for him that he had a chance with me again. Unfortunately, this was not the last of it. I learned a valuable lesson during this time about the tricks of the enemy: that he is persistent and will never stop trying to bring you back to where God brought you from. Since the enemy was so persistent to keep me bound, it was my duty to remain diligent and stay in the Lord's presence.

One day, I had a life-changing experience at church. I very vividly recall a particular church service during which the Spirit of the Lord spoke very heavily to me. At the end of the service, there was an altar call that challenged every man who had felt the prompting of the Holy Spirit to come forward. My heart began pounding incredibly hard in my chest, and I could hardly breathe. I did not want to go to the altar because I was afraid of what others might think about me. At this time, I had not shared my testimony and kept what God was doing in my life to myself. By His Spirit, the Lord told me to get up and go to the altar. I did not want to, so I resisted. After a few moments of wrestling with God, I felt my body rise up on its own, and as soon as my feet were planted, I started running at full speed! My eyes were completely closed, and I was running at full speed like a track star. I was literally having an out-of-body experience. I remember that my pastor began to glorify God for my breakthrough. Interestingly enough, something else began to happen. I started going out of control and expressing erratic body behaviors. I heard my pastor shout, "Hold him!" Several of the male ministers came and grabbed both of my arms as I continued to express erratic body movements. I also was screaming to the top of my lungs in a loud screech. Through all of this, my eyes were still closed, and I could only hear. The next thing I knew, my pastor came and laid hands on me, and immediately, I felt what I know to be an evil spirit in me come from my belly and through my mouth like vomit. It was very similar to *The Exorcist* movie! I fell to the floor and had no strength to get up. It was the scariest thing that had happened to me in my life at this point. I could not move, talk, or see. As I lay on the floor, the Lord ministered to me during this time. It was insane. When I finally was able to get up, I was terrified. I remained scared for about two more weeks, but then I started to feel different. I realized I had been delivered from the spirit of homosexuality! The spirit that had tormented me for years of my life was removed. I had never felt so light and free. The experience forever changed me! Through the remainder of my freshmen year through my sophomore year, I walked in a life of freedom in this area. Glory to God in the highest! He had set me free!

My sophomore year was a very pivotal time in my life. It was during this time that I learned more about the character of God and who He was. I started to walk more confidently in Him. While things were seemingly going well, there were still many areas in my life I needed to give to the Lord. Throughout my sophomore year, the Lord revealed to me that I had a hard time giving myself over to Him. I was satisfied with giving homosexuality to Him because it was not something I wanted in my life, but everything else was off limits. I still enjoyed other areas of sin. This revelation was given to me at a time when I had experienced a lot of hurt, disappointments, and betrayal in my life. I saw myself spiraling downhill very fast, and I was developing a bad drinking habit. It was extremely unhealthy, and I knew I had to do something about it.

My breaking point came when homosexuality began to find its way back into my life. I met a friend whom I had become close to, but I found myself contemplating being intimate with him. It was in this contemplation that I realized I was slowly falling back into my past life. Thankfully, I chose not to pursue that relationship. I knew there was only one thing that could help bring me out of my darkness. I heard the Spirit of the Lord speak to me and tell me to go to Bible study. So, I did just that. And it was in Bible study that the Lord began to stir me up. It was truly like fire was in my bones. My hands would shake, and heat would circulate through my body. It was a fire that I could not contain. At night, I would toss and turn because I could literally feel the Lord's presence burning within me. Then one Sunday morning, I went to church. That morning, the Lord's presence stirred so deep within me that as my pastor was speaking and preaching, I leaped to my feet and praised God with an undignified praise! I danced like David danced. I danced out of my shoes, my jacket, and my tie. The saints glorified God with me. Something special happened to me that day. I was filled with the Holy Spirit (Acts 4:31)! From this day forward, my life was forever changed.

Soon thereafter, I began to see visions and dreams. There were instances when I would sit in a church service and God would translate to me and show me things of which I had not dreamed. I began to move and operate in the power of the Holy Spirit. I laid hands on the sick, and they got well. I prophesied in His name. I spoke words of knowledge and wisdom. I spoke in the unknown tongues. I had never known these things until this point. It was all by the Lord's power. The Holy Spirit spoke to me in ways I had not seen. He quickly notified me to find a group of believers I could walk with to help me become strong in the faith. Although I was new to the faith walk and excited about ministering to others, my sophomore year came with many personal hurts, disappointments, and betrayals. These personal hurts, disappointments, and betrayals came mainly from friendships. Many people that I thought were my friends proved to be otherwise. Those whom I had trusted to be by my side had abandoned me, and I was bitter with these experiences.

At the time, my attitude was to operate alone in my faith. But God spoke to me and let me know that this could not be, because my ministry was to His people. Therefore, I found a Christian fraternity that consisted of young men that were like me, ready and willing to seek the will of the Lord. For the first time in my life, I had brothers who loved and supported me. They truly wanted to be my friend, and most of all, we were brothers in Christ. We prayed together, we fasted together, and we sought God together. My faith and vigor grew exponentially with this support and fellowship of my brothers. God healed a lot of hurt in my life that I did not know was there.

One crucial aspect of the fraternity that was pivotal to my walk with Christ was sharing our testimonies. Up until this point, I had not shared with anyone what God had done for me. Everything you have read thus far was a secret kept between God and me. I was incredibly nervous not knowing the reaction I would get from others when I told them I used to live a life of homosexuality. Being involved in church all of my life, I knew that talking about homosexuality was never an easy discussion to have. It was taboo. The first person I told my testimony to was the most incredible young man. I remember shaking with fear as I told him about what the Lord had done for me. To my surprise, he praised God for His goodness. He actually celebrated the Lord for bringing me out of darkness. His response was critical for me. He will always be part of my testimony! It is because of this young man that I am able to have the courage to write this very book about my testimony. His response sparked a confidence in me that I had not known before. From that moment forward, I told my testimony to every active member in my fraternity and eventually to every single person who would give me the opportunity to speak with them. I had the joy of the Lord. Thankfully, my testimony was generally well received. This fraternity was an unexpected blessing in my life. If it was not for this fraternity, I would not be the believer I am today. Being involved in this fraternity also provided me with other opportunities to be involved in the Christian community on my campus. I got to serve in freshmen orientation retreats to pray and lead new students into the presence of God and more.

In my junior year of college, I met a young man who eventually became my best friend and still is today. I include him in my testimony because God used him to reveal many things in me and about my character. He was the first person in my life to become close to me in my personal world. I think we often form surface relationships with people we meet. We eat with them and fellowship with them, but we don't often really get to know who they are. My best friend showed me many things about my personal character and ways that it needed to be developed. God was developing character within me. It is simply not enough to be anointed; you must have character.

The first thing that God used my best friend to do in my life was show me genuine love. I had not loved another man the way I loved him. It was not perverted or odd. It was truly genuine. It was the first healthy relationship I had with another male, as well as the closest. This relationship allowed me to open up and love people the way God loved me. I was no longer afraid to love with my whole heart. By this point, life had beaten me down, but I have always had a sensitive heart toward people. The Lord was breaking down walls in my life that had been built for many years. He then began to reveal things in me that were not so great. The love for my best friend also opened the door for idolatry. I idolized our relationship because I was afraid of losing it. Our friendship meant the world to me, and in many ways, it was too good to be true. I would do anything for him as long as it did not go against the will of God. But I placed our relationship above God, and it caused many issues between us. I became obsessive and controlling because I was scared that he would eventually grow tired of me and I would no longer be the best friend in his life. This was a new insecurity to me but something that reached deep down in my life. While I understood that my parents loved me, I have always felt to some extent that I was not loved. Because of the verbal and emotional abuse I had experienced throughout all of my life until college, I believed I had not experienced a love that made me feel wanted, needed, and accepted. For the very first time aside from God, I felt that someone wanted, needed, accepted, and loved me completely. I meant so much to him, and no one had ever made me feel this way. Through many mistakes, I became aware of my flaws and realized I was using my best friend to fill a void in my life that I did not allow God to fill.

Another lesson my best friend taught me was how to love others the way they needed to be loved. In my relationships up to this point, I wanted to make people do what I wanted them to do. I thought my way was the best and absolute way, and I did not consider others. I learned how to accept someone for who God made them to be. I learned how to care, share, and support those close to me, rather than use manipulation. I also learned how to pray and fast for someone close to me, especially when they did not choose the path that was best for them. These lessons would be helpful for me in the future for things that were unknown to me at that time. My best friend was my first interaction with a deeper understanding of what it meant to be in relationship with others through Christ. The relationship with my best friend also provided me with an extended family that would support me in years to come.

The summer after my junior year was an exciting one. I was about to be a senior, and I was going to be working at a Christian camp and ministering to youth. Not to mention, I was able to make money to pay for future plans to travel abroad. I was living the best days of my life. I found the camp was full of other college men and women who were as excited about God as I was.

There were many things I remember vividly from my first few days there. The biggest thing I remember is being shown a video specifically about homosexuality. The video told us that if we had struggled with homosexuality at any point, we could not work there. I couldn't believe this. Why was my struggle greater or much different from any other? Sure, I understood the various things that had taken place over the years, but I did not feel that this was the best approach. As a result, I struggled to reveal my testimony to anyone, but I could not hide what God had done for me simply because it made someone else uncomfortable.

Later, we had a men's small group, and I mentioned my testimony. To my surprise, it was well received. Many guys confessed to me privately that they also struggled with same-sex attraction. I knew my story was too great to be kept secret, even though I knew it would come at a great cost. The final week of training, we were asked to share our testimonies to our leadership through writing. I knew if I shared my testimony, I would be fired. But I couldn't lie about what God had done for me. What He did was too great! On my first day of camp, I was called into the office with a group of male leadership and was asked to immediately pack my bags and leave. I had no time to make arrangements, no chance to say goodbye to my friends. It was hurtful, humiliating, and wrong. I had nowhere to go and no plan. For the first time in my walk with God, I suffered persecution and was misunderstood for my testimony. Not to mention, this was by people of God that I had expected to lift me up. What I had thought was a blessing appeared to be destruction. I was hurt beyond belief.

This was an opportunity for the enemy to move. He fed me lies about my testimony to cause me to doubt if it was real and if I would ever truly overcome homosexuality. I felt misunderstood as I had when I was a child. I was now homeless, moving from house to house. My future was not so bright anymore. My relationship with my family was not doing so well for a variety of reasons, and now I had no way of finding funds to pay for my expenses for my senior year. I had given up so much to serve the Lord with this camp. But through all of the trials and heartbreak, God kept my mind. I honestly do not know how I made it through this time. God never gave up on me. I wanted to go back to homosexuality since I was rejected, but God wouldn't let me go.

I couldn't give up on what God had done for me because others, even Christians, could not understand me. The enemy meant to use this as a chance to silence me from speaking about my testimony. This book would not have been written if I had allowed him to be successful. God used what the enemy meant for evil to strengthen my resolve in what He had done for me. I was ready for my future, forgetting what was behind me. I found my joy in God alone.

My senior year was filled with nothing but God's glory. I never walked with such joy of the Lord as I did then. It was amazing to be known as a man of the Lord. I could not believe I was someone who people would call a man of God. This was strange to me because I had always thought people who were on fire for God were strange. I was okay with believing in God, but being on fire was another thing all in itself.

My final year of college was filled with not only His glory, but many tests. During the second semester of my junior year, the Lord had spoken to me and told me to go abroad. So, I applied to go abroad, although I did not have the grades to do so. However, God made a way for me to attend because it was His will for my life. During this time, God challenged me in many ways. I was alone with no one to lean on. I could no longer lean on Christian circles, accountable partners, church services, and any of the things that we do in the Christian world for support. I was soon reminded of a prayer that I prayed in the Spirit to God. I asked the Lord to remove all crutches and to bring me to a place where I could only depend on Him. Thus, the Spirit of the Lord led me overseas. I was in a place where no one around me knew I was a Christian. This was an opportunity for me to let loose. I was surrounded by everything fleshly—sex, money, drugs, alcohol, and more. There were more temptations here than I would have preferred. Nevertheless, I chose to serve God, and many times, this was not well received. I learned to depend on the Holy Spirit more than I had ever done so in times past. The lessons I learned in this season were to prepare me for my last season in college.

The transition back to my home country was slightly challenging. However, I was thankful that while overseas, I did not lose my heart toward God. I quickly reengaged in the Christian community and even took on some leadership roles in various Christian student organizations. Between getting settled back in at home and my involvement in different organizations, I felt myself struggling to maintain my intimate relationship with God. While I was involved in Christian duties, my relationship with God began to slack little by little. By this, I mean my time in the Word of God and in prayer started to become less over time. It wasn't long before the enemy was ready to move in.

I don't even recall how we met, but I came in contact with a guy who wanted to meet me based on the things others had spoken about me and my walk with the Lord. I didn't know at that time he was sent on assignment by the enemy. He mentioned that he had heard so many great things about me and wanted to meet up to hang out. In my mind, I was very honored and also naïve. I did not know then that not everyone wants to be your friend. Eventually, we met up, and immediately, my spirit became uncomfortable. I knew something wasn't right about this individual. However, I was extremely confused because he was talking about God and quoting scriptures. At this point in my walk with God, many people I met were genuine about their walk with God. I had not met many who professed God outwardly but were not in relationship with Him privately. Over dinner, I felt a heavy sense of sexual attraction between us. The way he looked at me was incredibly sexual but also demonic. I soon asked him about his testimony, and he revealed that he also struggled with homosexuality. But the interesting point was that he had not dealt with it, and he mentioned it so quickly as to not

39

spend time on it. I knew then this was a setup by the devil. Immediately, I ended the night and took him home. He began to open up to me and wanted comfort. I knew I couldn't give in because it would lead to a place I wouldn't be able to come back from, so I sent him on his way. After reflecting on the situation, I was nervous because this was the first time in years that I had been confronted face-to-face with this sin. This was during my third year of deliverance from homosexuality.

I was thankful to pass this test! When my feet had almost slipped, God kept me. Despite all of these things, the Holy Spirit had warned me to be very careful about maintaining my relationship with Him. Greater trials were coming that I would need to be ready for. I knew I should keep close watch on these things, but it was very hard, as I was finishing up my last year of school and embarking on a new journey to graduate school. Indeed, I found myself falling back into sexual temptations that I had defeated and wavering in my walk. However, I was able to seek God's forgiveness through repentance and make it through my mess-ups until graduation. I still had hope for a bright future. The next chapter discusses my post-college journey and the experiences that were extremely critical in my walk with God and for my future.

Summary and Key Themes

My college years were full of highs and lows. At the start, I fell into sin because I wanted to be accepted and loved. It was the first time I felt people genuinely liked me for who I was. I thank God for my spiritual upbringing, which prompted me to find a church. My church was my saving grace and allowed me to experience God in ways I had not before. Eventually, God took a hold of my life, and I turned over homosexuality to Him, but my journey was not without its fair share of ups and downs. Ultimately, it was a choice I had to make, whether I would follow God or follow the way of the world. Each day was a challenge to walk away from something that had become the very being of who I was. But I had a new identity in Christ, and it allowed me to walk in the Spirit and not the flesh. I began to live a life of freedom in Christ Jesus.

Key themes discussed in this chapter are:

- **Deliverance.** My college career did not even get the opportunity to see much of the sin of homosexuality as I had hoped. God had a plan for my life, and it included deliverance. God delivered me from the strongholds of homosexuality. There is deliverance for all who want and desire it. If you want it, then you can have it.

- **Spiritual Warfare.** That which we see in the natural world is directly connected to the war waging in the invisible spiritual world. I learned this very quickly as I began to fight with the Word of God the things that I could not see. I began to literally speak the Word of God to anxiety, depression, homosexual desires, lustful desires, and more. Of course, I applied practical applications to overcome my struggles, but practical applications are not enough. I had to understand that there is a war going on that I could not see (Eph. 6:10-20).

- **A relationship with God.** During this time, I learned foremost that we must have a real and authentic relationship with God. It is not enough to give over portions of our lives to Jesus; we must give it all to Him. Developing a relationship with God was one of the best things I could have ever done.

Key Scriptures

And when they had prayed, the place in which they were gath-
ered together
was shaken, and they were all filled with the Holy Spirit and
continued to
speak the word of God with boldness.
Acts 4:31

I appeal to you therefore, brothers, by the mercies of god, to present
your bodies as a living sacrifice, holy and acceptable to God,
which is your spiritual worship. Do not be conformed to this
world, but be transformed by the renewal of your mind, that
by testing you may discern what is the will of god, what is
good and acceptable and perfect.
Romans 12:1-2

...because the gospel came to you not only in word, but also
in power and in the Holy Spirit and with full conviction . . .
1 Thessalonians 1:5

Be sober-minded; be watchful. Your adversary the devil
prowls around
like a roaring lion, seeking someone to devour.
1 Peter 5:8

CHAPTER 4

My Graduate School Years

Graduating from college was one of my proudest moments. I had always dreamed it would happen, but I never expected to find God through all of it. Now my path was taking me to graduate school and a completely new environment with new challenges. I cherished every moment I spent at Texas A&M because it was where I found God. However, I was ready to see what new adventures God had in store for me. I was a Christian full of fire and zeal. The Holy Spirit was sending me on assignment into enemy territory. By this, I understood that where God was sending me was under attack by many evil spiritual forces that were unseen. There were many things I would have to encounter, such as homosexual preferences, lust, drunkenness, wild partying, pride, atheism, and more. I was sure nothing could stop me with God on my side.

As it turned out, I was not prepared for this experience at all. It was extremely challenging for me because it was much different from my old college. There were many conservative students at my old school, but most believed in God, even if it was not always evident in their lifestyles. The Christian community on campus was extremely large, and I was able to flourish as a believer. At my new school, things were much more difficult for me. I had always been very bold in asking others about their faith and if they believed in Jesus, but I found out very quickly that this approach did not work there. I was immediately outcast for being a Christian, as most people I met either did not believe in Jesus Christ or did not have positive experiences with Christianity. What I found most alarming was the rejection I faced even within the Christian community on campus. Many people thought I was over-the-top and radical in my faith. I discovered many Christian students were not living a life dedicated to Christ and struggled with the many temptations on campus. Encountering these obstacles began to weigh heavily on me. I have never felt as much an outsider as I did during this time. And it sent me down a dark path.

In this new environment, I realized I needed to hold on to God more than ever or I would be swayed by the temptations all around me. Remembering what the Holy Spirit had spoken to me about slipping away in my resolve with Him, specifically through prayer and spending time in His Word, it became evident what I needed to do—find a church home and be with strong believers. As I began my search, I knew the Lord had heard my cry and every step I took was ordered by Him. Before starting school, I had compiled a list of churches in the surrounding area based on recommendations from people at my current church. Interestingly, when I visited the churches from my list, I found that either they had closed or I had missed the service. I was so disappointed. So, I Googled a church near me and called to see if they were still in service. To my surprise, they were. As I made my way to this church, God spoke to me and told me to not judge the outside appearance of the building but the authenticity of the Spirit. The day I attended this church, I immediately knew this was where the Lord had placed me. I now called Greater St. John's Church my home. As I previously mentioned, I have chosen to not use real names for places and people for the most part; however, because this church was so significant in my testimony, I have chosen to list it by its real name.

Greater St. John's was truly my anchor during this six-year period of my life (Heb. 10:25). This church did more things for me than I could ever fit in this book. Thus, I have chosen key moments that were critical to my testimony. During my time in graduate school, I had periods when I doubted what the Holy Spirit was saying to me. I questioned whether it was real or true. I allowed the opinions of others to overshadow what I knew deep down to be true. I ignored the prompting of the Holy Spirit and allowed myself to be swayed by past sins in my life.

The first challenge I encountered was with a young lady. She was on fire for the Lord, and I was extremely attracted to her spirit. I had never met a girl as on fire for God as she was. I remember asking the Lord if she was the one He had for me. He spoke very clearly to me in this conversation and told me she was not the one. In my heart, I was okay with this, but I still wanted to at least be friends with her. I had been taught in my early walk with Christ about being intentional with the opposite sex and guarding their heart as well as my own. As much teaching and instruction as I had, I made many mistakes in this relationship. I thought I was strong enough in my faith to maintain a healthy friendship with this young lady, but I soon discovered that was not the case. We crossed many boundaries spiritually with each other that we should not have, and we created a soul-tie. At its core, a soul-tie is a spiritual connection that one has with another person that was designed to draw you closer to God. However, many times, these soul-ties are not created with the intent of a deeper relationship with God and are often destructive and ungodly. Soul-ties can be formed biologically, physically, emotionally, spiritually, and mentally. The soul-tie that I had with the young lady previously mentioned was emotional and mental. While we never did anything sexual, we allowed ourselves to be vulnerable with each other. Eventually, after many hard conversations and slip-ups, we ended our relationship. This was extremely hard for me because she was the first young lady I had feelings for since my deliverance. Losing her friendship put me on a dark path.

I began to backslide in my personal convictions and fall back into committing sins I thought I had overcome, many of which were sexual. These sexual sins eventually led me back to homosexuality. My sensitivity to the Holy Spirit began to lessen, and old sinful desires rose within me (1 Thess. 1:5). I would often place myself into sinful situations with other men who I thought were genuine in their pursuit of friendship with me, only to discover there was more to it. A specific example that will always remain with me was a young man I met during a Christian hangout. We immediately connected, and he shared his testimony with me. Things got really emotional with us, and before I knew it, we became extremely physical with each other. We soon began sleeping in the same bed together. Though we did not have sexual interactions, I knew I was living in complete sin. I could not believe how fast and easy it was for me to fall into such sinful actions, especially with another Christian. I felt so disappointed in myself because I had been successful for five years and was so easily brought back down. The strange thing was I enjoyed living in sin with this young man. But God had done too much for me to go back to what He had called me away from. I called out to God in the midst of my sin and asked for him to move this man out of my life because I knew I did not have the strength to do so. My flesh loved where I was, but my spirit was in agony because of my sin.

My church played a huge part in this because we were small in number but mighty in spirit. They could sense I was living in sin, and they loved me back to where I needed to be. They called out sin but did so by allowing me grace and time to get to where I needed to be. I recall a moment at church during this time when a lady began to operate in the Spirit of prophecy. She called me to the front of the church and told me I was beginning to backslide in my faith walk with Jesus. She demonstrated what this looked like by stepping back inch-by-inch until she was far from her original spot. I had not seen prophecy carried out in this manner before, but I knew it was God. After much prayer, God ended my relationship with this young man. I was free from a sinful situation that had been difficult to overcome. I had to take a deep look at myself and learn from my mistakes.

Unfortunately, even though I began to make progress moving away from my sinful actions, it seemed I was on a roller coaster. I thought I was okay and doing much better, but I kept finding myself in one situation after another. These were often due to naivety and not being watchful in the Spirit. Because of old insecurities and the need for approval, I fostered situations I did not want to be in. Sin has an interesting way of creeping into our lives and bringing us down. Once it has penetrated every area of our lives, it is extremely difficult to get it out. Every day, I found myself struggling to live holy and live the kind of life I knew I could.

I learned many things from my mistakes. I learned I must be watchful for the tricks of the enemy who seeks to devour God's people (1 Pet. 5:8). I had to protect the anointing that God had placed over my life. My intentions were not always to sin against God, but the enemy had plans for me that I was often too ignorant to recognize. I learned very quickly I must always stay connected to God through prayer, fasting, and time in the Word. My lack of doing so made room for separation and disconnect from the Holy Spirit, who would warn me prior to any attacks from the enemy. I learned that I must always examine my own heart (Psalm 139:23–24). I often gave space for the enemy in my life knowingly and unknowingly. The heart is deceptively wicked and can lead us down a terrible path. While I would like to blame everything on the enemy, my mistakes were often made with my help. I learned a sad truth—not everyone who screams the praises of the Lord is truly for the Lord. I was often prey for many "Christians" who were being used by the enemy. However, this was not the case with everyone. Some men I encountered were struggling as I was to fight this sin but had not received victory for themselves. Like me, they wanted to live a different life, but the grips of sin are strong indeed. However, I know through my own testimony that the power of God is so much stronger than the grips of sin. I've learned to be wise about my interactions and the consequences of sin. I was determined to not be defeated by my past sins.

Also during this time, I struggled with the idea of marriage and my insecurities about getting married. Throughout my time as an undergraduate, my main focus was on God, and I wanted to fall more in love with Jesus every single day. This was after I tried to pursue women immediately following my deliverance. As I began to walk more in the calling that God had on my life, I found I loved the freedom of singleness. I was able to do anything and everything God wanted of me without any attachments. I grew fond of this idea and was content where I was. But despite the joy of being single, I felt an underlying insecurity about getting married. At one point in college, I had a conversation with some friends about possibly getting married. I knew it would be hard for someone to want to be in a relationship with me because I had come out of homosexuality and was open about my deliverance. Most people with whom I shared my testimony rejoiced and praised God for what He had done; however, wanting to be in a relationship with me was a completely different story. It was a hard reality I had to face within the Christian community. My experiences have shown me that Christians are not always the best at accepting the hard truths and realities that some people encounter. It is much easier to praise God and dance around the hard realities of life. But I had been fortunate enough to be around true believers who believed God for me when I did not have enough faith to believe for myself.

I wanted to believe I would one day find a wife, but my reality made it seem unlikely. That reality consistently weighed on me. My final year of graduate school came with many questions. What was my next step? Where was I going to find a job? My peers faced the same questions. But for me, the most prominent question at this point was, will I ever find someone to love? Looking at social media can really affect the way you view life. It appeared that everyone but me was finding someone and getting engaged. I was serving God as best I could and trying to be faithful, but it seemed there was little to no hope for me. My church played a critical role in my life during this time. Early on, I had shared my testimony publicly with my church. Of course, they praised God for His goodness and would always speak life to me and encourage me that God would bless me with a wife someday. Those words were truly life to me in this season. But my journey toward deliverance was not a perfect one. I had messed up, fallen, and almost given up at times. And I was now twenty-four years old, and people were beginning to ask questions about dating, children, et cetera. This made being single that much harder. By this time, all of my friends were happily married, and many were having their first child. Here I was, not married and living a life of singleness. Despite the challenges I was faced with, I had to remember that waiting time was not wasted time. I had to wait for God's best and nothing less.

Eventually, I graduated and found a full-time job, but I continued to find myself in a difficult place. I was now a young working professional with no family close by. The people I met who were single and around my age were not trying to live a life of holiness. The life for a single young adult was one of partying, sex, drugs, and unhealthy relationships. My church was the only thing I had to hold on to. I did my best to make the most of my career by traveling, speaking at conferences and other venues within higher education, and pursuing leadership opportunities. After a year of being a full-time professional, I decided to apply to a doctoral program to get my PhD. After a few rejections, God blessed me to get accepted. During my first year of school, I had one prayer—I prayed to God that He would allow me to get married before I graduated. To be honest, this wasn't really a spoken prayer but more of a thought in my mind and heart. God knows even the secret prayers of your heart. When I didn't think God was listening, He was. God was working behind the scenes in my life. The end of 2015 was critical for my testimony because it marked the sixth year of my deliverance. This meant 2016 was the seventh year of my deliverance. The number seven is extremely significant in the Bible—it's referenced a total of 860 times. In the Bible, the number seven represents completion and perfection, both physically and spiritually. For me, 2016 was a year of completion, spiritually and physically. I believed that God was going to complete everything I had encountered with homosexuality. For me, this meant God wasn't going to stop at simply delivering me from that lifestyle; He was going to give me a wife and even children one day. I truly believe my seventh year of deliverance signified the completeness of growth and time that I needed for God to do His work in me. No matter how much I fell, God said the steps of a good man were ordered by the Lord (Psalm 37:23). Though he may fall seven times, he rises again (Prov. 24:16). I couldn't see the manifestation of the miracle, but I believed by faith.

Summary and Key Themes

The years between my promise and my destination were some of the hardest I had in the faith. I had to learn very hard lessons to prepare me for my future. At times, I felt I would not make it. I wanted to throw in the towel. God was faithful to me through all of my mistakes and hang-ups. Everything the enemy meant for evil, God used it for my good.

Key themes discussed in this chapter are:

- **Wavering in my faith and conviction.** I struggled a lot with my faith because I surrounded myself with people who made me doubt the convictions the Lord had given me. We must be careful who we surround ourselves with because the influence of the enemy is tempting. Always surround yourself with wise counsel.

- **Insecurity in the promises of God.** I had many opportunities to not trust God or to believe that He couldn't do the impossible in my life. I have learned and am learning that by faith, I can receive everything that God has for me. I must be faithful and wait on the manifestation of His promise.

- **The year of completion.** This was spiritual symbolism for my life that God was completing His work in me. God had delivered me for seven years of my life.

Key Scriptures

Search me, O God, and know my heart! Try me and know
my thoughts!
And see if there be any grievous way in me, and lead me in the
way of everlasting!
Psalm 139:23-24

Be watchful, stand firm in the faith, act like men, be strong.
1 Corinthians 16:13

Do not quench the Spirit.
1 Thessalonians 5:19

Not neglecting to meet together, as is the habit of some, but
encouraging one another, and all the more as you see the
day drawing near.
Hebrews 10:25

Be sober-minded; be watchful. Your adversary the devil
prowls around
like a roaring lion, seeking someone to devour.
1 Peter 5:8

CHAPTER 5

My Marriage

This chapter is dedicated to my journey to marriage. My marriage is more than a Cinderella story; it is the manifestation of God's glory! Significant things happened during this time. I entered my seventh and eighth years of deliverance. And most importantly, I met my beautiful wife, who has changed my entire life and has been the fulfillment of my testimony.

Year of Completion

As I mentioned in chapter four, 2016 was my year of completion. In January 2016, I was in a church service when the Holy Spirit began to operate through prophecy. The Holy Spirit was using a young lady to bring prophecy to God's people, and the lady called me up to the front of the church. Up to this point, I was hoping I would not get called upon. She spoke to me by the Spirit of God and said, "Terrance, there is something you desire from the Lord, but you have not asked Him." In my head, I thought, *I feel like I have everything I need from God and don't know what to ask for.* Immediately upon thinking this, she said, "And you are probably thinking to yourself, I feel like I have everything I need from God and don't know what to ask for." I knew then this was surely the Lord. She pointed out to me that there was *one* thing I wanted from the Lord but was afraid to ask for it. The only thing I could think of was that I wanted a wife. But I did not feel like I should ask for such a thing from God because He had already done so much for me in my life. The young lady continued to speak to me and told me to put the very thing I wanted from God in my mind and then praise Him for it. My church, being who they were, glorified God with me, although they had no idea what I had asked Him for. It was a great day, and I was so encouraged!

Of course, I was extremely optimistic and knew that my wife was coming in the same month. I was so excited that I did not remember to prepare my mind, because after every victory is an open opportunity for the enemy to try to steal the very thing God promised to you. We are usually the least guarded after a victory. I wish I could say everything was easy from this point on, but it was not. I experienced some of the hardest challenges with homosexuality that I had ever experienced before. The attacks on my life were intense and direct. No matter the mistakes or the challenges I barely escaped from, I had to hold on to the promise of God. It seems that right before you experience a breakthrough is often when all hell will break loose in your life. I may stumble, I may wobble, but I won't break as long as I hold on to Jesus!

As I was believing God for the miracle, I had to seek Him for instructions. This would take trust and yielding to the Holy Spirit on my part (Phil. 4:6). As you could imagine, I was anxious to walk into the blessing God had for me. But there were still some things God had to do in me before I could receive this blessing. This was clear to me when I noticed that God allowed the enemy to test me in areas I thought I was solid in, to reveal where I really was in Him. Despite learning this, I continued to not be still. Rather than wait on God, I was too busy trying to make the promise come to pass. Over the next year, I encountered several women who I thought may be my future wife. Each time I would ask God, "Is she the one?" to my surprise, the Lord did answer me, but it was not the answer I wanted to hear. The answer was, "No. Be patient." I allowed my friends, who were not walking with the Lord, to give me advice about dating. They would say things like, "How do you know she's not the one unless you try?" Or, "You need to put yourself out there to know if it's right." Sadly, I did try to pursue relationships with these women. One by one, they failed. Eventually, I got fed up with trying to pursue women and gave my will over to God. I was angry because I knew none were the woman God had for me. No matter how much I tried to lie to myself or convince myself that one of these women and I could possibly work, I knew there was something missing. My anger and disappointment almost led me to pursue a sexual relationship with a woman from my past who I knew wanted a relationship with me, but I stopped myself because I knew it was not godly.

I had hit my breaking point and knew I needed help. I called my best friend and one of my brothers in Christ to pray with me about this situation. After our prayer, I felt much better. I knew what I had to do. For two weeks, I blocked out all distractions and chose to pursue God completely. It was in those two weeks that I heard the Holy Spirit speak to me. He told me to "get ready, she is on her way!" I remembered a saint from my church telling me to pray for my wife and to ask God for the things I wanted in a wife. Honestly, I did not really think I knew what was best for me, nor did I want to leave it to chance. So, my only prayer for my wife was that she loved the Lord as fiercely as I did. I was terrified of marrying the wrong person and even more terrified of marrying someone who did not share the same passion and love for God as I did. This was of extreme importance to me. I knew I would have to be honest with my wife about my testimony and what I had been through. I could not hide what the Lord had done for me, and I wouldn't sacrifice hiding my testimony to be in a marriage.

Year of New Beginnings

January 2017 marked the eighth year of my deliverance! I was more than excited for this year. As I mentioned in the previous chapter, in Scripture, the year of seven marks the year of completion and fulfillment. The eighth year is also significant because it is the year of new beginnings. While in my place of prayer, I heard the voice of the Lord tell me the woman of faith He had for me was near. This was exciting news to hear, but I was definitely skeptical. After an entire year of disappointments and failures, I was not quite so sure of this message from God. I wouldn't say I was in disbelief, but I wanted to be careful and be sure that I heard this from God.

At the beginning of the third year of my doctoral program, I walked into my first day of class with much excitement, only to find there were no seats available. Then I spotted the one vacant seat. You might have guessed by now that this seat was next to Aundreia, my wife. Of course, at the time, I did not know this. I sat down, and we began talking. I introduced myself, and we started to get to know each other. I mentioned how much I enjoyed cooking, which is something I mention to everyone because I am extremely passionate about cooking and believe wholeheartedly that food connects the world. As luck would have it, one of the requirements of this class included pairing up with someone in the class for a project. Wouldn't you know, Aundreia and I became partners and exchanged phone numbers. But once the class session was over, we said our good-byes until the next class session. I did, however, send her a word of encouragement from my daily Bible devotionals, but she did not respond. I was very sad about this. I also invited her over to my apartment for a big dinner that I was having with friends, and sadly, she once again did not respond. I thought for sure she was not interested in being my friend.

At our next class period, I brought my famous peach cobbler for everyone to enjoy. At the end of class, there was some cobbler left over, and I did not want to take it home. To my surprise, Aundreia offered to take it home to give to her brothers. It was then we began to talk more intentionally, and we discovered we were both passionate about Jesus. I believe it was in this moment that the Lord began to knit our hearts together. We also came to realize we were in the same circle of friends but somehow had never met. I told Aundreia I was planning to get one of my wisdom teeth removed and was terrified based on the horror stories people had told me. She told me she would pray for me and would check up on me. I was truly thankful for her prayers.

On my way home that night, I asked the Lord more about Aundreia. Was she the woman I had been looking for? But I still didn't feel ready to get involved in a relationship because of my year of disappointments. The next day, I got my wisdom tooth removed. Without delay, Aundreia sent me a text checking in on me. Not only did she send me a text that day, which was a Tuesday, but she sent me a text to check on me every day for the remainder of the week. As we continued to text, I knew that our hearts were becoming more knit together. We began to ask more questions to get to know each other. Eventually, we discovered we liked and were interested in each other. I must say, at that point, I was very direct and intentional about things I wanted to know. I was fed up with playing games with women and relationships. So, I asked Aundreia questions about marriage, children, faith, credit score, and more. By the way, this was only our second week knowing each other. This may seem pretty fast, but I was not about to play games and beat around the bush. If she did not have intentions on being married, then I wanted to know this. After talking through all of these things, we came to realize we both wanted our relationship to be intentional with hopes of marriage.

I was so excited about this. I had never been in a dating relationship with anyone before. But I knew that before I could officially ask her to be my girlfriend, I had to be honest with her about my testimony.

I was terrified to no end about telling Aundreia about my past. This would be the deal breaker. I knew if she could accept my past and believe that God had really delivered me, then she was definitely the woman I had been searching for. After stressing out about this and receiving some wise counsel from my friends, I decided to tell her everything. And believe it or not, she was fine with my testimony and even celebrated the fact that I had the courage to tell her. I will never forget the specific words she said to me: "There is nothing you can say that would change the way I feel about you!" When I heard these words, I cried for about two weeks. I also found I could hardly eat because I was so thankful to God. I knew from this very moment she was the woman of my dreams. We officially started dating on Thursday, February 9, 2017. This may sound crazy, but I bought her ring that following Monday. I knew she was the one for me. The rest is history. We made sure to do everything in decency and in order. We met with our parents, family, and friends because our community was important to us. The best part of this process was that the favor of the Lord was upon us. People would weep when they met Aundreia because they knew that God's love and favor was evident.

Our wedding was a special time for us because we wanted God to be the center of everything we did. It was the most blessed time I could have ever asked for. I believe my marriage was the completion of my testimony! This does not mean that God doesn't have more for me, but I believe God will complete what He started. God gave me a wife who is so strong in her faith that she can be married to a man with such a peppered past as I had. Not only that, but she always encourages me to continue to walk in the call that God has on my life. Maybe one day she will write her own book.

We have now been married for almost two years, and it has been nothing but pure joy to be with someone who loves me completely. This is not the end of my story, but I thank God that He gave me the strength to share my story with you. I pray that this book ministered to you and gave you a new sense of hope and perspective.

Summary and Key Themes

The purpose of this chapter was to provide a sense of closure for my testimony. While my story is still being lived, I believe God finishes what He starts. In this chapter, I highlight many spiritual victories, one being the significance of my eighth year of deliverance. The number eight in Scripture signifies a new beginning. I spoke about my marriage and chose to highlight it to provide hope to those who feel God cannot completely turn life around and give them a brand-new start. Not only will God provide for you as His redeemed one, but He will also give you more than you could ever dream.

The key theme discussed in this chapter is:

- **The manifestation of the promise.** I believed by faith that God would be faithful to bless me with a wife if it was His will. By faith, I had confidence that if I asked anything according to His will, He would hear me (1 John 5:14–15). Not only did God redeem me, but He gave me a brand-new start and blessed me with a wife, which was something I had given up hope on. He will finish the work He started in you.

Key Scriptures

He who finds a wife finds what is good and
receives favor from the Lord.
Proverbs 18:22

Being confident of this, that he who began a good work
in you will carry it on to completion until the
day of Christ Jesus.
Philippians 1:6

Do not be anxious about anything, but in every situation, by
prayer and petition, with thanksgiving, present your
requests to God.
Philippians 4:6

Conclusion

I thank God I have the privilege to share my story with you. Though this may be unconventional to say, I one hundred percent believe homosexuality is a sin (Lev. 18:22; Rom. 1:26-27; 1 Cor. 6:9-10; 1 Tim. 1:9-10). However, I do not believe this sin is any greater than other sins listed in the Bible. My deliverance from homosexuality was not without proper understanding of my situation. As I sat under the teachings and conviction of the Holy Spirit, I was able to be freed from the bondage of my sins. I had many sins I was walking in. However, for the purpose of this book, the sin I highlighted is homosexuality. Sin can be described as (1) overstepping the law, the boundary between good and evil; (2) the act that is inherently wrong, whether explicitly stated or not; (3) departure from right; (4) failure to meet divine standard; (5) trespass; (6) lawlessness; and (7) unbelief (Rom. 3). Sin also leads to death, and I was surely dead on the inside.

As I mentioned in the book, I wanted to believe so badly that I could make peace with my sin, believing that maybe it was my portion in life. I wanted to accept that God made me this way and I would live my life as such. But this was a lie from the enemy! I was made in the image of God, and fearfully and wonderfully made at that (Gen. 1:27; Psalm 139:14). There was a small piece of me buried away that knew I was not walking with God and knew there was deliverance, joy, peace, and more for me. I did not have enough courage or strength to walk out of my sins. I needed more. I had to understand sin and its destructive power. If you do not view homosexuality as a sin, then you will not be able to walk in the deliverance and freedom that God has for you.

Understanding and acknowledging homosexuality as a sin is the first step. We must also repent of our sins. Once I understood the goodness of God, His patience, kindness, love, and plan for salvation, it led me to repentance (Rom. 3:4). As I began to accept the idea of a new hope, I learned about my union with Christ and how His death and resurrection provided me with everything I needed for the deliverance from the power of indwelling sin. My union with Christ meant the sinful man within me died with Christ, and my new life was a result of His resurrection (Rom. 6:4). What did this mean? It meant for me that I no longer had to be controlled by my sin (homosexuality), nor did I have to submit or give in to the lustful desires I had. I did not choose to struggle with homosexuality or the lustful desires that accompany it. We are born into a sinful world, and each one of us struggles with our own lustful desires. But our faith and hope in Christ is powerful enough to overcome any and every sin or temptation!

When I truly accepted Christ, I was given the Holy Spirit. I learned that the more I sought after the Holy Spirit like a hidden treasure, the more sin had no place in my life (Rom. 8:13). The Holy Spirit enabled me to kill my desires for same-sex relationships. It was not easy by any means, but the Lord was teaching me how to fight. Ultimately, I had to make an active choice to choose Christ. There was a lot of influence from my friends and others who encouraged me to not change just because of what people preach and teach at church. But this was not the work of any human, but of the Holy Spirit. I knew I had to answer the call. I made many mistakes and failed throughout my walk, but I could not give up because God was not going to give up on me. Whether I messed up once or multiple times, it did not change the deliverance God had given me.

If you are praying for someone in your life who struggles with sin, never stop praying. If you have dropped the prayers you once prayed for this person, pick them back up. Never underestimate the power of prayer, because somebody prayed for me. My mother's prayers were critical in my deliverance as well. Keep praying because you never know what God is doing.

My deliverance does not mean I now hate or crucify anyone in the LGBTQIA+ community. There is no way I could hate the very people I once fellowshipped with. My goal for this book was to provide a narrative that is different from what exists and to share what God has done in me. I pray my story was encouraging and uplifting. Thank you for taking the time to read about the miracle God performed in my life.

Key Scriptures

So God created man in his own image, in the image of
God he created him; male and female he created them.
Genesis 1:27

I praise you, for I am fearfully and wonderfully made. Wonderful
are your works; my soul knows it very well.
Psalm 139:14

Or do you presume on the riches of his kindness and forbearance
and patience, not knowing that God's kindness is meant to lead you to
repentance?
Romans 3:4

We were buried therefore with him by baptism into death, in
order that,
just as Christ was raised from the dead by the glory of the Father, we
too might walk in newness of life.
Romans 6:4

For if you live according to the flesh you will die, but if by the
Spirit you
put to death the deeds of the body, you will live.
Romans 8:13

CPSIA information can be obtained
at www.ICGtesting.com
Printed in the USA
LVHW010046230620
658655LV00005B/817